NAME	SUBJECT

Printed in Great Britain
by Amazon

58540659R00088